The Secret
of the
Yamas

The Secret of the Yamas

A Spiritual Guide to Yoga

by
John McAfee

Woodland Publications

Credits

Editor: Jinny Ruths, Touchstone Publications
Production Manager: Pamela Jones
Cover Design: Jesse Epting
Design and Production: Graphics West, Inc., Colorado Springs, Colorado
Printer: Kendall Printing, Greeley, Colorado

Copyright 2001 by Woodland Publications

Associate Publisher: Rogue Amazon Publications

2000 Arapaho Street
Woodland Park, Colorado 80863
EMAIL: support@woodlandpublications.com
WEBSITE: http://www.woodlandpublications.com

ISBN 0-9711569-0-5

DEDICATION

This book is dedicated to the legacies of
Charles Darwin, who showed us the infinite
beauty in the flowering of life;
to Ramana Maharshi, who pointed to the
silence in which all things exist;
and to Jiddu Krishnamurti, who shed such
brilliant light on the source of
ignorance and suffering.

CONTENTS

CHAPTER
ONE

Introduction

In this age of technology, mass media, ever-expanding entertainment and sophisticated marketing that keep us on the move and perpetually busy, the journey of self-discovery is often lost or relegated to the category of mysticism. Yet, without a firm understanding of ourselves—who we are, how we relate to the world and why we do the things we do—we cannot possibly live life to its fullest. We have explored ever-widening aspects of the outer world: both physically, in terms of the world's geography and composition, and theoretically, in terms of the scientific disciplines. We have plumbed the depths of the oceans, trekked through distant wilderness, climbed every mountain and taken tentative steps into space. We know the workings of distant solar systems and can predict the movements of subatomic particles. We are unraveling the genetic make-up of life. But

how many of us have sought out the source of our own desires? Discovered the root of fear? Explored the mechanics of envy, loneliness or greed? Or noticed our past conditioning that restricts our freedom of action in virtually every situation? Surely these things impact us as much as any knowledge of the external world.

Self-discovery, or self-awareness, has occupied a place in human history since the beginning of recorded time. From the Delphic oracle of Greek mythology that cryptically advised supplicants to "Know thyself," to modern-day gurus of self-awareness, the quest for self-understanding is a thread of continuity in the human condition. Shakespeare used the absence of self-knowledge to explain the chaos surrounding King Lear, declaring: "He hath ever but slenderly known himself." And the founder of every great religion has at some point directed his or her followers to look inward.

So we could ask ourselves: why do we find ever more pressing reasons to throw ourselves into the external world and avoid facing ourselves? Why do we seek larger entertainments and increasingly sensual activities? Why do we jump from one cause to another, one ideal to another, one relationship to another? Why are we so powerfully drawn to television, or books, or hobbies, or companionship? Why do we feel discomfort when all distractions have ceased and we are left

with nothing but ourselves? These are important questions. Until we ask them and burn
for the answers, all the explanations in the
world will be of no avail. We can intellectually
know an answer by hearing it, and can talk
sensibly about it and sound knowledgeable.
But there is no truth to it for us until we have
discovered the answer within ourselves.
Without self-revelation the answers are only a
formula of words with no true connection to
our experienced reality. And without that we
will never know that flowering of life in which
total understanding dawns.

Yoga originated at least 2,500 years ago,
with the purpose of creating self-awareness in
the practitioner. Patanjali, who first docu-
mented the organized science of yoga, states
in the opening lines of his famous yoga
treatise: "The union of the various parts of the
mind is gained through control of the mind,
and then the perceiver comes to consciousness of himself." This statement clearly indi-
cates the major purpose of the practice
of yoga as understood by Patanjali: self-
consciousness. This purpose has been
downplayed over time until now it is hardly a
consideration in the practice of most teachers

and students. We are aware of yoga only as a technique to gain physical strength, flexibility, or increased health. And indeed these are potent side effects of the practice. But that is what they are: side effects. To focus on these largely insignificant manifestations (compared to its intended focus) is to miss the point entirely.

As with every other aspect of modern life, we have emphasized the material, external aspects of yoga, to the detriment of its deeper potential. Patanjali describes a comprehensive system of yoga in which the asanas, or physical postures, play only a small role. Yet they have been inflated beyond proportion and given the authority of time and custom by each successive line of yoga masters through the ages. The asanas are important, of course, and the mastery of them creates great powers in the individual. But without an understanding of their value in relation to the whole of the yoga practice it is like having a fine automobile while understanding nothing of driving or the automobile's purpose. We may appreciate sitting in the car and perhaps showing it off to our friends, but we are missing its true value.

The hope for this book, for those who are interested and are willing to ask and answer difficult questions, is that it helps point out the true value of our yoga practice and place it in a context that increases our understanding of ourselves, our relationships and our actions.

CHAPTER
TWO

The Yamas

Patanjali described an eight-limbed yoga that, if practiced properly, is said to bring the practitioner to a state of self-awareness. One of the eight limbs, or paths, is asanas, the postures, and this is the aspect of yoga with which we are most familiar. Yamas, or the five conditions of behavior, make up a second limb. These conditions are non-violence, non-stealing, chastity, absence of greed, and truthfulness. The yamas have been loosely compared to rules of behavior that exist in nearly every religious or social philosophy. These rules are generally considered logical guidelines for an orderly society, or as personal guidelines for shaping and improving the individual self.

As personal guidelines, the yamas are believed to act as mechanisms of change, as a method of transforming the individual from one state to another. Through the practice of

these guidelines we strive to become something greater, more spiritual or happier. We
believe that we can discipline ourselves inter-
nally, and through discipline change into
something else. We can certainly discipline
the body to become stronger and more flexi-
ble. But can we discipline our psyche so that
we change arrogance into humility, for example, or create love where hatred exists? Virtually every religion and social code encourages
us to love our neighbor. But can we, through
the power of will, create love? We can certainly act love. We can constrain our behavior
and work to avoid hostility with our neighbor.
We can smile and say appropriate words and
conform to expectations; we can cultivate outward tolerance. We can pretend all manner of
behavior. But how do we discipline ourselves
into a state of loving? Anyone who has observed themselves in an effort to become loving will see the futility of this approach.

You cannot learn to love your neighbor
through discipline, force or willful effort.
Love flowers truly only when the heart and
the mind are in perfect union. And this union
itself cannot be brought into being through

discipline or effort. It comes into being on its own, spontaneously, as we will see.

Any effort to conform to a formula or live by prescribed rules is in effect living through imitation. We are imitating the actions of those whom we believe to be holy or superior

or enlightened, and through this imitation we hope to become like them. But in reality, we become narrow and limited. We face each infinite moment of life through the filter of these ideals, with the result that creative thought and spontaneous action cease. As our range of thought and action narrows, we become more separate from others, more opinionated, more arrogant, even though we believe we are becoming more holy. And the end result is the opposite of what we had hoped to achieve. Imitation is not being.

You can test this process in yourself. If you desire a slim figure, for example, you will eventually notice your opposite desire for fattening foods. It is a reality within yourself. You can overcome it for a time, but doing so merely creates a conflict between what you are and what you want to become. You may in fact succeed in slimming down, but the opposite desire will remain with you. It may show up in some other way such as irritability or antagonism, or perhaps the original desire will resurface with renewed force and once again you find your eating out of control. The desire is part of you, existing regardless of your discipline. If you look deeply you will see the same is true of arrogance, greed, envy and any other quality that you might seek to eradicate or change.

You might point out that discipline is necessary and effective in learning a profession or a skill, or that progress in construction, science or technology is impossible without discipline. But these are all processes in the external, physical world. Here we are dealing with the subjective world: the world of desires, fears, hopes, securities. These emotions operate very differently than the principles of engineering, for example.

When we look closely at our attempts to discipline desire, we inevitably find another desire. If we desire to please our boss we may have to work on weekends. If we simultaneously desire to please our spouse we want to be home on weekends. We clearly have two desires in conflict, as all desires ultimately are, with each attempting to eradicate or control another. Thus we have desire attempting to discipline itself, to eradicate itself. But this process merely strengthens desire through the energy we pour into it.

Is it likely then that Patanjali had discipline or exercise of will in mind when he described the five yamas? Was he directing us to take arms against ourselves and battle our baser natures? Perhaps advising us to turn our backs on such impulses and hope they go away while we attempt to cultivate replacement virtues? Assuming none of these approaches is what Patanjali intended, then what is the significance of the conditions of behavior that he set down? What are we to make of them?

CHAPTER
THREE

Non-Violence

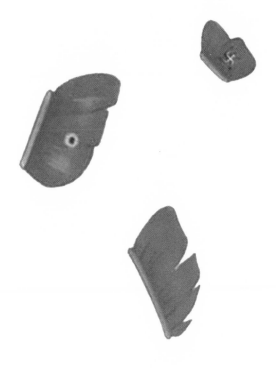

The first of the yamas is *ahimsa,* a Sanskrit word translated alternatively as non-injury, non-violence, harmlessness or absence of hostility. It appears as a central point not only in Patanjali's Sutras, but also in most of the world's major religions, most of which have practiced its opposite on many occasions as evidenced by the religious basis of dozens of wars fought in the past few years.

It should be obvious that the condition of non-violence would never need to be raised if we were not in fact violent people. We might reject that conclusion on a personal level, while recognizing violence in others, but if we are honest with ourselves we will see that violence is an integral part of our nature. We may not openly assault our neighbors, or take out our frustrations on innocent bystanders, but nevertheless we are filled with fears and suspicions, that mold our behavior. We perceive threats to our security, real or imagined, and feel hostility. We enjoy a secret pleasure

when people who have done wrong are punished. We have divided the world into uncountable divisions of individuals and groups that we like or dislike, approve of or condemn. We do violence every time we attempt to sway someone to our point of view, or dissuade someone from a course of action that we, in our arrogance, feel is wrong. Violence is the attempt to impress our will or beliefs onto others, or to prevent others from infringing on our own ideals and principles.

What are we to do then with this violence, which is part of our being? If we attempt to overcome it don't we commit violence against ourselves? We struggle against our own violence, attempt to subdue it, contain it, eradicate it, and this effort is violence. This internal struggle is a war with our very nature. We demand non-violence, strive to discipline ourselves, and in the process we strengthen the root of violence within us.

Please don't simply accept or reject these statements. Look for the struggle taking place within you, and observe what happens to your own violent nature as a result of this struggle. Your own observations can be the only judge of the truth.

If we cannot eradicate our internal violence through an effort of will, then what can we do? What process will free us from the bonds of violence? Yet, in asking this question we are placing the cart before the horse. Do we understand the full nature of violence—its internal causes and the full impact of its outward effects? Do we understand the conditions that give violence its energy and power? Do we know its source, its root, or the mechanism that sustains it? Do we in fact know what we want to eliminate? If not, then any attempt to change it cannot possibly succeed. If you only know the surface effects of violence then that surface is all you can deal with. Any cosmetic changes will produce only surface results. The underlying violence will continue unchanged.

Thus, before we can truly effect any change, we must first delve into our violence, find its root cause, understand its workings, and fully see its impact on the world around us. Only then are we capable of true change.

The first step in understanding our violent nature might be the observation that violence is stimulated whenever our security is threatened. We have built complex walls of relationships, ideals, financial arrangements and religious beliefs, behind which we hide from change and uncertainty. We arrange our days to minimize threats to the structure we have so painstakingly constructed. We keep the fear of hunger at bay by storing up wealth. We comfort ourselves in the face of death with religious beliefs that promise the perpetuation of our individuality. We hold off loneliness by clinging to relationships, even at the expense of our true natures. We desperately seek continuity, and continuity is a fragile condition. The infinite flowering of life is a constant assault on the barriers we have constructed, and individual violence is the result.

Most of us would like a formula to end violence, a set of instructions for understanding our own violent natures. This desire is natural; we want to be led, assured, guided. But such a solution is a trick of the mind. No one can lead you to yourself, and there is no formula for self-discovery. These things are distractions, momentary occupations that keep the mind from perceiving what is plainly visible. Our violence is a fact, as factual as the page on which these words are printed. To see the root of our violence we only need to look. If we are fully aware of violence as it is happening, and observe, without judgment or distraction, then in that full observation the root of violence is revealed, and in that understanding violence evaporates. Then the duality of violence and its opposite cease to be an issue.

CHAPTER
FOUR

Non-Stealing

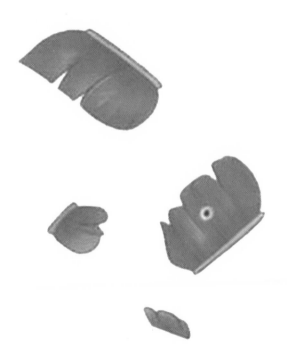

The Sanskrit word *asteya* literally means non-stealing, but many translators use the phrases "absence of jealousy" or "absence of envy" to more accurately convey what they believe to be the spirit of the word. The distinction is of little consequence, for delving into the act of theft inevitably brings us to the issue of jealousy. We want what others have, for whatever reason, and theft is one of the results. If we are jealous and do not steal, the urge may manifest as resentfulness, anger and indignation, and eventually we feel aggrieved. This grievance may reveal itself in subtle or overt ways; at the least our mistrust and suspicion have stolen the harmony of the relationship.

What then is Patanjali's implied instruction to us? He simply names the word *asteya* as one of the yamas. "Yama" is loosely translated as "form of constraint." No other clarification is offered. As with non-violence, the application of will power or other discipline will never free us from jealousy and envy. In the attempt we may indeed end up acting the perfect imitation of someone free from the bonds of envy, but we will have done so by creating a rigid formula of behavior and thereby destroying spontaneity of action. Our ability to meet life anew at each moment will be further crippled. The futility is evident to any who try. An attempt to willfully create an internal characteristic merely creates or expands its own opposite. In the effort to cultivate non-envy, we strengthen envy. Like violence, envy is our reality. We are jealous, envious and resentful, and that actuality will not go away by turning our backs on it.

Why do we envy others? We envy because we compare. Don't accept this blindly, but consider. We perpetually compare ourselves with those we consider lesser or greater, creating sophisticated structures of comparison. Our workplace contains our superiors and inferiors. Our neighborhood has both wealthier and less wealthy inhabitants against whom we measure our own worth. Our occupation is more or less desirable than

others. Our spouses are more or less attractive, our children smarter or not as sharp. We are knowledgeable or ignorant, stronger or weaker, powerful or powerless in comparison. We divide and classify the world and then compare ourselves to it. With each division we separate ourselves even more from the rest of humanity, and we become isolated. Whether we consciously perceive this isolation or deny it, it is a fact with most of us. We have created it through divisiveness and it is a part of us.

Because of this isolation and its accompanying emptiness, we do not live fully, and we crave fulfillment. We long to become something better or greater than we are, and hope that this becoming will provide us the fulfillment that we lack. If we are ignorant, we hope that knowledge will give us a complete sense of living, and we envy those who are more knowledgeable than ourselves. If we are poor, we think that the accumulation of wealth will provide fulfillment, and we envy the rich. If we are unattractive or friendless we believe that fulfillment lies in being attractive or having friends. We accumulate in an effort to fill our emptiness and are perpetually jealous of those who already have what we want. When we attempt to become something other than what we are, then we must forever have more. We must keep accumulating for we are in a never-ending state of becoming something better.

But this becoming better, or greater, is nothing more than an attempt to escape the reality of our emptiness. We cannot create fulfillment through effort any more than we can create non-violence through effort. We can only unravel this mystery by probing beneath the lack of fulfillment and finding its cause—our habit of dividing the world into comparative pieces. And beneath that is our original division of life into the duality of "myself" and "the rest of the world."

CHAPTER
FIVE

Chastity

The Sanskrit word *brahmacharya* is usually translated as chastity or continence, and most commentators stress sexual abstinence (or at least sexual fidelity) as the focus of this yama. Indeed, the issue of when, where, with whom and how often to have sex, or whether to have sex at all, has become a central problem for most of us. But isn't it a surface problem? The real question is not whether to indulge in sex or to be celibate, but why sex has taken such an important, central role in our lives. We have inflated its importance beyond any rational reason. We think about it, plan for it, indulge in elaborate schemes to obtain it. It is the source of transitory pleasure when we have it, and prolonged suffering when we are deprived of it. It is misused and misdirected. But despite its inflated importance, the problem of sex is only part of a larger problem.

The spirit of *brahmacharya* lies far deeper than the simple sexual problems most of us experience. A more appropriate translation may be "not being sensual," for sensuality, not sexuality is the core issue. We experience life through our senses—touch, taste, sight, sound and smell—and sensuality is the root of all desires. That is, it is the memory of sense experience that activates desire. For example, we experience the sight of a beautiful sunset and the joy of its pure beauty infuses us. What happens next? We want to repeat the experience, to relive the pleasure of that vision again and again. It is the same with all of our senses. We divide our sense experience into pleasurable or painful, beautiful or ugly, and we flee from the painful and cling to the pleasurable. We create formulas for living that minimize the painful sensations and maximize the pleasurable sensations.

But what happens to the original joy we experienced at the sight of a sunset? The joy was uninvited, a spontaneous response to beauty; but we grasp the experience and try to hold it, to repeat it. We wait for the next sunset and hope for the blossoming of that beauty, and when it comes it is not the same.

We have reduced the spontaneity of joy to the sensuality of pleasure. Beauty and joy occur when we are in the moment, when we are not anticipating, hoping, expecting. When we willfully attempt to create a feeling through excitation of the senses, we are no longer in the moment. Instead, we are attempting to manifest a remembered experience and repeat it. We abandon the possibility of spontaneous joy and instead search for pleasure, which is mere excitation of the senses.

The challenge then is to return to a spontaneous way of living that allows us to meet every moment of life anew. Attempting to shut down our senses is an obvious absurdity

and cannot help us. We must see, hear, smell, touch and taste in order to exist and relate to the world around us. Our senses are our doors to perception. Some religious disciplines advise us to restrict sensory inputs, such as limiting food types to flavorless fare, or advocate sexual abstinence, or require an austere sensual environment. But these are merely artificial, contrived restrictions that limit the natural flowering of life. Constraining the senses does not remove the problems of sensuality. Desire, which is grounded in the senses, will not cease by simply limiting the objects of our perception. If we do constrain our sensual input, then our thoughts will take up the overflow. Our thought process has its own sense capacity in the powers of inference and projection; thus thoughts can be the root of pleasure as much as any of our senses. And while we may have some say over the austerity of our food intake or our surroundings, we will be challenged indeed to exercise the same control over our thoughts.

Artificially limiting ourselves will do nothing to address the root problem—our desire for pleasures. We can replace the pleasure of the flesh with the pleasure of ideals, of dreams, or of superior spirituality. And they are all the same. We have simply moved the sensuality of the body into the sensuality of thought; the desire is undiminished.

So shouldn't we search out the cause of our need for sensual pleasure rather than shutting down the instruments that gratify that need?

What is the root cause of our need for pleasure? If you watch yourself carefully, you will see that the desire for pleasure begins with an image. We may feel sexual desire for someone who is not present, for example, and if you are aware you will notice that the desire comes with some image of past sexual experience with the person, or an image of what the sexual experience might be like. These images are created by memory. Even an image of some future experience is a composite of past similar experiences projected into the future.

Memory is the repository of the past, which is where most of our living takes place. We have divided life into past, present and future, and this division, like all of our divisions, removes us from the fullness of living,

from the mysterious unknown and unknowable movement of life that is the source of all beauty. If we observe ourselves in action, we will see that our lives are a process of constantly becoming something. We use the past to create the future through action in the present. We want something, or we want to be something, or we want to change something—thereby changing ourselves. Our vast store of memories creates a working formula for achieving some desired result, and we act based on that formula. But by living in the past or the future, we limit our capacity to act. The present is merely an opportunity to mold the future or to replay some past experience. This division of experience into time has created our difficulties. While we need chronological time, or time by the clock, in order to catch planes or get to meetings, the artificial creation of psychological time—that division of life into past, present and future, is an illusion. It is the source of our constant striving to become, instead of timeless being. The past exists only in memory, and the future is merely a projection of past memories. Now, this moment, is all there is.

We have the capacity for change. Not the change of becoming, which is no change at all, but the fundamental change of being: the change that brings us to understanding and to the full flowering of life as lived in the present moment.

We have traced sensuality through pleasure to its root in memory, which is the past. And living in the past is the source of psychological time, which separates us from ourselves. What can be done to free us from this morass? We have ourselves created psychological time. We are living in it. Every action, thought and feeling is a result of it. We experience it, taste it, smell it, and live it. If we cannot resolve this dilemma ourselves, how can anyone else resolve it for us?

Most of us want a guru, someone to lead us, assure us, direct us. But self-discovery can only occur in relationship to the present moment, and that relationship, composed of our actions, thoughts and feelings, is itself the guru. We are at every moment capable of looking at ourselves. For example, we all struggle with sexual issues. We expend our energies indulging in sex, or we deny our urges and are in conflict. But have we looked at what sex means in our lives? Have we

peeled back the layers and observed our sexual energy in action, while it was moving, flowering, or withering? Can we perceive, not just intellectually, but with our full hearts and minds, the root cause of our distorted desires? To do so requires simply willingness and courage. No signposts or instruction booklets are needed. The answer is there within us, waiting to be uncovered.

CHAPTER
SIX

Non-Attachment

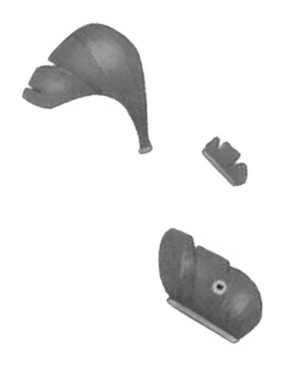

Most commentators translate this yama as "absence of greed," but *aparigraha*—the word Patanjali uses—has its roots in *pari* + *grah,* which means "to grasp onto," or to be attached. A better choice might be "non-attachment," although the distinction matters little, as greed is merely an attachment to the idea of "more."

As with each of the previous yamas we ask: Can Patanjali have meant for us to cultivate the quality of non-attachment? Did he mean for us to give away our possessions; abandon our relationships with people, things and ideas; and live with little or nothing? Perhaps he meant for us to foster an attitude of indifference to the things about us, so that they have no control over us. Or for us to let go of the things we cherish most, in order to experience the full impact of our attachment.

We should recognize immediately that we cannot will non-attachment into existence. No discipline, formula or process can create the quality of non-attachment. If we give away all of our possessions, wear rags and roam the streets, we have merely traded our attachment to things for an equally debilitating attachment to the ideal of non-attachment. We become proud in our lack of attachments; we feel superior, smug, above the rest of deluded mankind. And we will have restricted our already small existence even further through self-imposed and cruel constraints. We will have shut the infinite possibilities of life even further from our selves.

Even in cultivating an attitude of indifference to things, the most we can achieve is merely an imitation of indifference. And if we were successful, such indifference would only further isolate us from the rest of life.

We want to cultivate non-attachment, yet we generally know little or nothing about attachment. We know that we are attached; our love turns quickly to possessiveness. We cling to financial success, to our cars, televisions and toys. We are attached to ideas, political views, religions, neighborhoods, and nationalities. We clutch at our fading youth, our knowledge and our personal identities. Yet, until these attachments are understood, until we discover and explore their root cause, any attempt to create non-attachment will further strengthen the source of attachment.

The essential question is, why are we attached to anything at all? Attachment is rooted in our craving for continuity. We feel secure in the fragile construction of our everyday existence: the sameness of our jobs,

homes, regular activities. We have built walls to keep out fears and uncertainties, chaining ourselves to a narrow circle of the known. We feel safe in the continuity of our self-constructed environments; we identify with both the external environment of our homes and jobs and the internal environment of our ideals and beliefs. This identification helps us live the illusion of self-perpetuation, which is what continuity is really about. It is ourselves that we wish to make continuous. We vaguely perceive the reality of death and hope for personal immortality in spite of it, clinging to beliefs of afterlives, or reincarnations, or whatever offers the hope of personal continuity. And because we see nothing in life that is naturally permanent, we create an artificial environment. In a world of continuity we can more easily hope that the individual personality might also continue. But in this process, we have once again removed ourselves from the flow of life in which continuity has no real place. The craving for continuity invariably creates attachments, which become the stones of our personal prisons.

This realization gives rise to the next set of questions: What is this individuality that we are so desperate to perpetuate? Who is the "I" that seeks self-continuity? What exactly are we attempting to make immortal? Invariably, the answer to these questions is the "I" of the past, the "I" created in memory by the process of thinking. It is the fragment of thought that divides the world into Me and Not-Me, Mine and Not-Mine. It is the ego. The ego craves immortality, and it is the ego

that creates our prisons of continuity through the mechanism of attachment.

This petty, fearful entity—this bundle of opinions, greeds and self-serving processes—craves permanence. But immortality can never be achieved as long as the ego functions. Immortality springs into being with the understanding and destruction of our self-imposed prison of attachments, when we embrace life in the fullness of each moment, with full acceptance of its mystery.

CHAPTER
SEVEN

Truthfulness

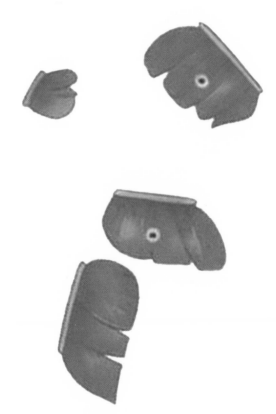

Truthfulness, or *satya,* is the final yama. *Satya* is translated as real, genuine or honest, and we generally take this Yama to mean that we should tell the truth. Telling the truth involves giving an accurate or complete account to others of what has happened, or what has been seen, heard or inferred, as well as accurately communicating one's thoughts, feelings and intentions to others. Inherent in this understanding is the assumption that we do not twist, alter or in any way transform the truth to suit our own purposes. Given that assumption, we must first ask: is such truthfulness possible? If we are 100% ready and willing to tell the truth, and are immune to consequences, can we even then tell the truth?

In the first part of truth telling—giving an accurate account of what has happened—we need to examine what we know about what

has happened. If you watch the process of perception in yourself, you find that every experience, act and sensation that comes to your awareness is first filtered through the background of your own conditioning. Experience is interpreted as it happens, and our interpretations are based on our unique system of beliefs, fears, cravings and anticipations and our past experiences in similar situations. For example, a fearful person walking into a ghetto might instantly perceive the rapid approach of a large stranger as a threat, while the stranger's intent might have been only to ask directions. Or when people in a room are laughing and appear to be looking in our direction, depending on our relationship to them and our current feelings about ourselves, we might perceive them as laughing about us. Somewhere in the process of perception the "might be" usually disappears and we store the information as an absolute: "they were laughing at me."

We may think that only the paranoid or unbalanced have such twisted perceptions, but we would be wrong. All of us are a bundle of opinions, beliefs and ideals that tell us what is "true" in people's intents; we overflow with fears and suspicions that tell us the "truth" of people's actions; we are full of pride and self-importance that tell us the "truth" of our own being. Surely telling these truths to others must be secondary to finding out what is fundamentally true ourselves.

We have all known the beauty of love, for example. But invariably, we soon begin to feel possessive of our love's object, and the possessiveness leads to jealousy, and then to anger; yet we continue to insist that we love.

But can possessiveness, jealousy and anger co-exist with love? Clearly not. They are mutually exclusive. The one destroys the other. Love eradicates all personal hatreds and jealousies, and where jealousy or possessiveness exits, love cannot. Yet, we still insist to ourselves and to others that we love. But if we look deeply enough, we will find that the root of our supposed love is our individual need for security, contentment or pleasure, or that it keeps fear or discomfort at bay. We use the object of love as a distraction against the unpleasant, or as a stimulus to pleasure. Cruel words perhaps, but please don't simply reject them out of hand. Look into yourself, without judgment or condemnation, but with simple observation. It is our condemnation that has originally created this inability to see the truth in ourselves.

We are violent and antagonistic, yet the filter of our perceptions allows us to believe that we are not, either through justification of our principles and ideals, or through blindness to our actions. We are envious and jealous, yet we perceive these qualities as ambition or a healthy competitive drive. We are filled with greed for material goods or even

spiritual progress, and as we accumulate we tell ourselves that we are being successful. We divide ourselves from others through vanity or feelings of superiority, and still pretend to be teachers and leaders. We filter everything that we know of ourselves through the sieve of our self-constructed self-image. And we create in our mind similar images of our spouses, children, neighbors, friends and enemies. In truth, all of our relationships are between our self-made image and the images we construct of other people. These images relate as if they possessed a life and reality of their own.

It should be clear that telling the truth to another person has little meaning until we first remove this veil of self-deception. It is ourselves we have deceived, and it is ourselves to whom we must first be true.

The question now becomes, how did this self-deception come about, and can we extricate ourselves from the illusions it has created? For if we cannot, then life is indeed a tragedy, certain to continue in suffering and ignorance.

CHAPTER
EIGHT

The Secret

Patanjali formulated and described eight limbs of yoga. We have addressed just one. Yet, as Buddhists are fond of saying, in the smallest fragment exists the whole. While we may not yet be ready, as a great Sufi saint once pointed out, to see the entire universe in a grain of sand, we can certainly see that if we seek out the very root of arrogance toward any one person, then we have found the root of arrogance toward all people. The same holds equally true for fear, hatred, anger, envy and any other quality of the mind. And if we approach the yamas with an attitude of serious inquiry, then we will find the whole of yoga within them.

When we look at the wide-ranging aspects of our violence, the multitudes of self-deception, the uncountable jealousies, lusts, and attachments, it may seem a daunting task to approach each one and uncover its core. But the root of each is the same. It is the root of ignorance. When that root is uncovered and understood with full heart and mind, then its power in any area of our lives evaporates. We are freed completely, immediately.

It is an illusion to believe that fundamental change requires time, that we must work diligently toward a goal and gradually become better, wiser, happier, and more spiritual. Such an approach uses the present moment as a tool to obtain future fulfillment; the present is used for planning, dreaming, working toward a result. Consequently, our lives are

lived in the future and we are in constant relationship to the past; and the field of life—the present moment—is missed entirely.

At each and every moment of our lives the root of ignorance is operating, and if we are alert we can see it in our relationships. All of life is relationship. We relate to people, things and ideas, and our actions reflect the tone and substance of each relationship. How we relate to money, to the ideal of love, to nature, to our concept of death, and to our spouse reveals, in the moment, the truth of ourselves. Planning and waiting for some future moment to see this truth is no more than avoidance based on fear. If you see even this fact with your entire being, then this new awareness also will lead you to the root of ignorance.

And what is this root? It is the ego. To the intellect, the ego is simply a convenient word that can explain all of our trials, and we are done with it. But to truly grasp the ego and see its reality as clearly as we see our face in the mirror requires more than intellectual knowledge.

The ego is the sense of "I" as separate from the rest of the world. It is our sense of

unique individuality. From this "I" stems the concept of "mine," and from "mine" ultimately springs all of our possessiveness, greed, envy, anger and dishonesty.

The "I" believes that it is unique and separate from the world. It believes it is capable of creativity and worthy of self-expression. But is it? We are, every one of us, conditioned by the past. We are driven by fear and drawn to the objects of our desires. We accumulate material goods, knowledge, talents and experiences, as do our neighbors. Our ideas are passed on from parents, and through education, books and the culture in which we are raised. We may pick and choose among these ideas according to personal preference and individual tendencies, but we did not create them. We are largely a product of society, and we in turn create society. As our nations, states or tribes are, so are we.

If we look at our religious beliefs, for example, on which we base much of our behavior, ideals and moral codes, we find that it was handed to us intact by our religious culture. None of us could seriously think that had we been born into a different religious culture we would nevertheless believe as we do now. Even when we swap our religious beliefs, don't we do so because of the influence of other people or other existing cultures? It is the same with all of our ideals, religious or otherwise. They have been created in us by society. Where now is our separateness, our uniqueness? At most we are all the same being with individual inclinations.

If we watch ourselves in action, we see that we are conditioned. Our actions are really re-actions. We re-act to each circumstance based on our memory, the repository of our past experiences. We are unable to meet each moment anew. If we are conditioned and re-active, then what place has creativity in all this?

On close inspection the ego appears neither as unique, nor as capable of creativity as we would like to believe. But what exactly is it then? What is its substance? Where does it reside? What maintains it?

The Ego

In the same way that we have separated ourselves from the world, creating the "I" as a separate entity, we have also divided our experience. We have divided thinking into the thought and the thinker. We have broken action into the act and the actor. We have fragmented perception into the perceiver and the object of perception. And in this process we have created the chooser and the choice. This thinker; this actor, this perceiver, this chooser is the ego.

But the thinker cannot be separated from the thought. Without one, the other cannot exist. The process of thinking is the only reality. The thinker is nothing more than thought dividing itself. Thought creates the thinker and attributes the qualities of choice, control and will to it. We have all experienced this reality but seldom look into it. Whenever we are caught up in a moment of profound beauty or danger, what happens? We momentarily forget ourselves. The individual "I" disappears and we are only acting, perceiving, being. There is no thinker or actor in these moments; no chooser exists. There is no center from which we experience. Only the experience itself exists. These moments are brief and infrequent, and we seldom take note of them or ponder their profound implications. Nevertheless, we experience them. And after

the danger has passed or we have filed away the beauty and hoped for more of it, the ego resurfaces and our thought process resumes.

There is no ego without thought. Experiment with this potential and you will experience the profound change that occurs when we are merely acting, perceiving, without the central point of the actor. The thinker, the actor, creates distance between itself and its object; it must do so to exist as a separate entity. And this distance is what separates us from the infinite movement of life, from the present moment.

Thought has divided itself and created the thinker. And for the thinker to continue to exist, our thoughts must continue their incessant chatter. Our thoughts are constantly organizing, planning, rehashing the past, judging, fantasizing. If we are aware, if we listen, we see that there is seldom a moment when the thought process is silent. It must continue. The ego demands continuance, permanence through thought, and this demand in turn leads to all the things we seek to eliminate.

Thoughts rise from memory, which is the repository of the past. The ego, being a fragment of thought, must then also exist in the past. It can project itself into the future and thus make plans for itself, but it cannot exist in the now. If we observe ourselves in

our relationships—through our actions, thoughts and feelings as they are happening—then we will catch a glimpse of the ego. In that light of awareness the ego will vanish, and in its place a profound silence will blossom. In that silence is all beauty. It is infinite, unknowable and not separate from ourselves. It is immortality.

APPENDIX A

The Eight Limbs of Yoga

Compiled by the Patanjali Maharishi in the Yoga Sutras, the Eight Limbs have classically been viewed as a progressive series of steps or disciplines which purify the body and mind, ultimately leading the yogi to enlightenment. They are listed here in classical form for purposes of historical interest.

The 8 limbs are:

1. **Yamas** The yamas or restraints are divided into five moral injuctions, aimed at destroying negative human characteristics. They are traditionally practiced and developed through self-discipline. The injunction is to practice the yamas in word, thought and deed.

- **Ahimsa** or non-violence
- **Satyam** or truthfulness
- **Brahmacharya** or moderation in all things (control of all senses). Also refers to celibacy
- **Asteya** or non-stealing
- **Aparigraha** or non-covetousness

2. **Niyamas** The niyamas or observances are also divided into five parts and compliment the conditions described in the yamas. These qualities are:
   - **Saucha** or purity—this internal and external cleanliness.
   - **Santosha** or contentment
   - **Tapas** or austerity
   - **Swadhyaya** or study of the sacred texts
   - **Ishwara Pranidhana** which is constantly living with an awareness of the divine Presence (surrender to God's Will)

3. **Asanas** Postures. These are designed to purify the body and prepare it for the task of internal disciplines.

4. **Pranayama** regulation or control of the breath. Asanas and Pranayama form the sub-division of Patanjali's yoga known as Hatha-Yoga.

5. **Pratyahara** withdrawal of the senses in order to still the mind.

6. **Dharana** concentration.

7. **Dhyana** meditation. It is a state of absorption in the object of meditation.

8. **Samadhi** the superconscious state. In Samadhi unity of self with all things is experienced. This is the state of consciousness where heart and mind have been unified and the Yogi is one with life.